The Mindful Way

Life Crisis

Catherine G. Lucas has experienced periods of profound psychospiritual crisis. Seeing the power of mindfulness to help her move successfully through these, she trained as a mindfulness teacher, qualifying in 2007. Among the many groups she has taught since then have been NHS therapists and, on behalf of the Ministry of Defence, soldiers returning from Iraq and Afghanistan.

Catherine is the founder of the UK Spiritual Crisis Network and the author of *In Case of Spiritual Emergency*. She is also the author of *Coping with a Mental Health Crisis: Seven steps to healing* and *Alcohol Recovery: The Mindful Way*, both published by Sheldon Press. She has been meditating for twenty years and offers retreats both in the UK and abroad.

Mindfulness titles available from Sheldon Press:

Alcohol Recovery
Catherine G. Lucas

Mood Swings
Caroline Mitchell

Anxiety and Depression
Dr Cheryl Rezek

Pain Management
Dr Cheryl Rezek

Compassion
Caroline Latham

Quit Smoking
Dr Cheryl Rezek

Keeping a Journal
Philip Cowell

Stress
Philip Cowell and Lorraine Millard

A full list of titles is available from Sheldon Press, 36 Causton Street, London SW1P 4ST and on our website at www.sheldonpress.co.uk

The Mindful Way

Life Crisis

CATHERINE G. LUCAS

First published in Great Britain in 2018

Sheldon Press
36 Causton Street
London SW1P 4ST
www.sheldonpress.co.uk

The author and publisher have made every effort to ensure that the
external website and email addresses included in this book are correct and
up to date at the time of going to press. The author and publisher are not
responsible for the content, quality or continuing accessibility of the sites.

British Library Cataloguing-in-Publication Data
A catalogue record for this book is available from the British Library

ISBN 978–1–84709–427–8
eBook ISBN 978–1–84709–428–5

Typeset by Falcon Oast Graphic Art Ltd, www.falcon.uk.com
First printed in Great Britain by Ashford Colour Press
Subsequently digitally reprinted in Great Britain

eBook by Falcon Oast Graphic Art Ltd, www.falcon.uk.com

Produced on paper from sustainable forests

For a world in crisis
May we find our way through with
mindfulness and compassion

Contents

Acknowledgements

Every night after we've turned the light out, my husband and I spend a few minutes sharing our appreciations and gratitudes for the day. Writing these acknowledgements provides me with a similar opportunity to reflect.

I'm grateful to Fiona Marshall and the whole team at Sheldon Press. It feels as if *Life Crisis: The Mindful Way* is particularly timely, so thank you Fiona for this opportunity to produce a title which is so greatly needed right now. A big thank you also to Deborah, Martina and Tina for sharing your valuable personal experience, which you were happy to have appear under your real names. Your stories of how mindfulness helped you and your loved ones in times of crisis are heart-warming.

I'd like to express my appreciation to Vidyamala, my mindfulness teacher. So much of my understanding of mindfulness comes from you. The absolute insistence on the central place of compassion within our mindfulness practice I owe to you, as I do the simple language of concepts such as primary and secondary suffering. Thank you.

Above all, I'm grateful for the beautiful quality of silence, the depth of the practice, that Swithin, my husband, and I have developed. It started out as a way of allowing me to focus and concentrate on writing (without hesitation, deviation or repetition, for fans of Radio 4's *Just a Minute!*) It then developed into something we both found so valuable that we have carried on long after the book was finished. So thank you, Swithin, for your deep respect for the silence, for all it holds and all it brings.

Finally, as I remind myself to keep surrendering and handing everything over to the Universe, I give thanks for having been guided to the writing life as a way of being of service. I give thanks for the opportunity to play my small part in helping to ease humanity's suffering.

Introduction

Life crisis comes knocking at our door wearing so many different hats. Invariably it will have an emotional and psychological impact. Even if the crisis takes the form of physical injury or illness, few of us are immune to the knock-on effects on our emotions and mental well-being. Whether your child has just received the diagnosis you never wanted to hear, whether your husband has just announced he's having an affair and wants a divorce, or whether your mother is nearing the end of her life, *Life Crisis* has something for you.

Whether your outer world has been hit by an earthquake or your inner world is crumbling into rubble, here you will find ways of soothing and supporting yourself using the principles and practices of mindfulness.

My story

In 2003 I went through a period of profound crisis. At a time in my life when, as part of a psychotherapy training course, I was doing deep healing work through one-to-one therapy, I was also engaging fully in my spiritual quest. As I turned 40, things came to a head. On a trip to Egypt, I experienced a week of intense psychospiritual crisis that left me completely incapacitated, physically, mentally and emotionally. In the shock and trauma my legs gave way and for a few days I couldn't even walk.

What I learned at that time was the power of mindfulness to help me cope, to get me through the worst. As I had been meditating for a number of years, I had already started to learn the skills of watching the mind, of being the 'observer'. As I followed the antics of the mind I began to see a relationship between my levels of fear and the kind of thinking the mind was engaged in.

Whenever my anxiety levels became really high, the thoughts and ideas would get more wild, more extreme, catastrophizing and distorting. This awareness helped me to step back a little, to unplug from the mind's cavorting, just enough to be able to get my feet on the ground once more. After the worst three or four days, in which I had to use a wheelchair, I was able to walk again normally.

That crisis turned my life around. It helped me to see how even the most extreme emergency can be an opportunity for growth and healing, for change and transformation. I came through, creating some very positive changes in my life.

When the opportunity to train as a mindfulness teacher came up, I seized it eagerly. I knew that this was exactly what I wanted to do. I had seen for myself the power of mindfulness to transform the most acute situations. Following that period of crisis I also organized a series of residential conferences on psychospiritual crisis, or spiritual emergency, and set up the UK Spiritual Crisis Network. I wrote my first book (*In Case of Spiritual Emergency*) and spoke at various events and conferences, including in the United States and at the Consciousness in Crisis conference at the University of Leiden, Netherlands. I was invited to contribute a chapter on a 'Mindfulness-based approach to spiritual crisis' to a German handbook on spiritual crisis. In 2007 I became one of the first accredited trainers of the mindfulness training school Breathworks. I've taught many groups since then, including NHS therapists and, for the Ministry of Defence, soldiers returning from Iraq and Afghanistan.

I'd been teaching for a couple of years when a close relative had a complete meltdown and turned to me in despair. She had been thrown out of her family home because of her drinking, and her life was spiralling out of control. It was becoming increasingly difficult for her to hold down her responsible job. One day, instead of going to work, she got on a train heading in the opposite direction, not knowing where she was going or where she would end up. I got a phone call out of the blue. She was at a train station somewhere, she barely knew where, and all she kept repeating, frantically asking over and over again, was 'What am I going to do? What am I going to do?' When I reached her at the station, she was suicidal. She could see no possible way out of the nightmare her life had become.

Over the next 48 hours I supported her in the best way I knew. Using mindfulness techniques, I constantly encouraged her to come into the present moment. Her greatest fear was about the future, so I worked at helping her simply to get through each moment, right now – to forget about the future for the time being. The only moment she needed to get through was this one.

I showed her how to come into the present moment through the physical senses and the body. I repeatedly brought her back to what she was sensing, what she was aware of in her body, physically. This is something we do when using mindfulness to transform crisis; we keep repeating, coming back to the same thing over and over again. We talk about 'working with the fear'. Because we can't just bring ourselves back into the present moment once and think 'great, job done'. The mind will spiral off again and again. As you can tell from my own experience, the greater the levels of anxiety and fear, even terror, the more the mind will spiral out of control.

My relative had no previous experience whatsoever of mindfulness, and yet within a couple of days she had successfully managed to come through her crisis. It helped that I had complete trust in the process, that this period of what looked like breakdown was in fact a breakthrough, allowing a whole new level of healing and growth. I also took her to my GP to get her signed off from work. For the first time she woke up to the fact that there were mental health issues underlying her drinking. That completely changed her perspective and, with the support of Alcoholics Anonymous, she has turned her life around. She has repaired her marriage and is once more a highly valued and respected member of her work team.

My relative's story attests to the power of mindfulness to help transform crisis. I had already known as much from my own experience, but this incident served to strengthen my conviction. Teaching mindfulness to those struggling with acute emotional and psychological pain has been hugely rewarding. Being able to give students the principles and techniques of the approach that will allow them to be with, and ultimately relieve, their suffering has been satisfying beyond words.

People who have participated in my mindfulness courses include someone caring for and supporting a close friend dying of cancer, women struggling with their grief after the recent death of their husbands, a young mother whose baby had been born with special needs and a man who, after his business had nearly gone under during the recession, had been forced to make many staff redundant, including people who had mortgages and families to support. The soldiers I taught returning from Iraq and Afghanistan were suffering from both post-traumatic stress and physical pain. Each of these individuals, from the young mother to the businessman, from the widows to the war veterans, was grappling with a different kind of crisis, a different kind of emotional, psychological or physical pain, yet each found relief through mindfulness.

I know crisis holds the potential for growth and healing, for change and transformation. My own experience and those of my relative and my students have shown me that. This has been a key theme running through all my publications and has been at the heart of my work for many years. After my first book came out, Sheldon Press approached me to write *Coping with a Mental Health Crisis*. Since then I've written *Alcohol Recovery*, also in the Mindful Way series.

This book

My work has always been motivated by a desire to alleviate the suffering of those going through personal crisis. I'm now starting also to turn my attention to how we cope with the current world situation, and this is reflected in Chapter 1. In our interdependent age, personal crisis and the global state of emergency are not as separate as they may seem.

Another key theme running through my work is that it is mindfulness which enables us to turn crisis into opportunity; it is through awareness that transformation is possible. So in Chapter 1 we also touch on how mindfulness helps us grow that pearl from the grit.

Chapter 2 looks at how mindfulness works, and here we start exploring some of its key principles. In Chapter 3 we consider the research evidence and developments in neuroscience which are now allowing us to understand just why mindfulness is so effective.

Part 2 of the book covers the practices themselves. In selecting and devising these I held two questions in mind: 'What are the main issues we're dealing with in times of crisis?' and the related question 'What do we specifically need mindfulness to help us with?' Here are my answers.

- We need to reach out for support and we need self-care and self-compassion.
- We need to be able to calm down, to reduce our level of arousal.
- We're likely to instinctively want to resist what is happening, so we need help to work with that resistance.
- We need to be able to cope with intense emotions, especially fear, and possibly physical pain too.
- We need to stay in the present moment, without dwelling on the past or catastrophizing about the future. In crisis, the only moment we need to get through is the present one.

You'll find that the practices in Part 2 address these needs. They are gentle, realistic practices for hard times, always with the emphasis on self-nurture. Please take good care of yourself; reach out for professional support if you need it. I would also encourage you to get as much support –

practical and emotional – as you can from family, friends, neighbours or colleagues. I will be by your side, holding your hand through the practices. With the right help, your crisis can be creative!

Part 1

Holding your hand

1

Transforming crisis

Trieste, Italy
The soup starts gently lurching from side to side in our bowls, as it would on an ocean liner rolling and pitching on the high waves. But we're not at sea. My little brother points at the ceiling. 'Look!' he shouts. The light hanging over the dining table is swaying slowly, eerily, from side to side. There's a strange, distant rumbling. My father dashes out to investigate, thinking maybe the central heating is exploding. Then it's over.

It was 6 May 1976 and an earthquake had just devastated Friuli in north-east Italy. What we felt in our home, some 60 miles away in Trieste, on what was then the Yugoslavian border, measured (at its epicentre) 6.5 on the Richter scale. It left nearly a thousand dead and 157,000 homeless.

We are bombarded daily by images of similar disasters. As I write, forest fires have swept across parts of parched Europe, destroying homes and habitats. Texas has just been ravaged by storms and flooding. The war in Syria claims civilian after civilian.

Things happen

These catastrophes are examples of what we might call 'primary suffering'. Things happen in life over which we have no control: we lose a loved one, we lose our livelihood, our relationship or our health breaks down. This is primary suffering. It is universal. A fact of life. Illness, old age and death are facts of life. Primary suffering is inevitable. Take a pause, take a moment to breathe into that truth. We need to meet it with love and compassion, with tenderness.

The problem is this though: we argue with life. We argue with the facts. We fight and resist, we kick and scream, we try to shore up our lives against it. We don't want our beloved to walk out on us; we don't want the grief of a miscarriage; we don't want to have to make decisions about turning off a life support machine. As Byron Katie, author and spiritual teacher, says, if we argue with reality we will lose, but only 100 per cent of the time. That hurts. Fighting with reality is painful. Resisting the inevitable brings a different kind of suffering, a more painful kind. This is what we might call 'secondary suffering'.

The good news is that we don't have to fight reality. There is a different way of doing things that hurts a lot less. While we can do precious little about primary suffering, about the things that just happen to us in life, we can do everything about secondary suffering. We can respond in ways that alleviate rather than exacerbate our suffering. How do we do that? Through mindfulness. Using this ancient wisdom we can find steadiness in the midst of our life's earthquake.

Everyone's crisis

This book is for everyone. For everyone living in the twenty-first century. Crisis is universal. It comes to all of us at some time, in some guise. Right now, because of the interdependent world in which we live, we are all experiencing crisis of global proportions. Our climate, our refugees, our terrorism and our economic well-being are all interrelated, inextricably and irrevocably woven together.

We know in our hearts that families in Syria are no different from our family. That is why the Syrian war impacts on us. When Texas experiences flooding we remember how hard local communities closer to home were hit by our own floods, whatever their scale. When locals and tourists are mown down in Nice or Barcelona, we remember terrorist incidents in our own country. Their crisis is our crisis.

I call this international state of emergency 'the dark night of the globe'. It is a collapse in systems, ecological, socio-economic and political. In terms of the dynamics of the process, the breakdown that holds the potential for breakthrough, it is comparable to the kind of crisis someone going through a mental breakdown or dark night of the soul experiences. (In my book *Coping with a Mental Health Crisis*, I explore in detail how every breakdown holds the potential for healing and growth.)

As the ice caps melt into the ocean, the same ocean that the Fukushima reactor continues to pour radio-activity into, we know that we ourselves have caused many of these disasters. Even the ones we think of as 'natural', like earthquakes. Petroleum and water, left untouched in the earth's crust, help to lubricate and smooth the shifting of tectonic plates. As we continue to extract more and more such materials through wells, leaving natural reserves depleted, we only exacerbate the incidence of earthquakes.

Turning towards the painful

Global crisis has a different impact on each of us. Either we turn and look the other way – keeping ourselves busy in our denial with all the trappings of life: kids, job, mort-gage – or we freeze in fear, overwhelmed by feelings of powerlessness, of lack of control. Alternatively, we seek to numb ourselves and our feelings through umpteen addictions, from outright dependency on alcohol or drugs (including prescribed ones) to overworking, overconsum-ing, or even over-talking.

Global crisis is the primary suffering. It is a fact. The myriad ways in which we run, hide from, dodge and deny this reality are the secondary suffering. As hard as we might try to ignore it, as hard as we might try to busy ourselves with everyday life, there is no denying the reality of our collective situation. We cannot pretend any longer it is not happening. We can no longer ignore it.

There comes a point when a person with terminal cancer can no longer truly deny she is going to die, can no longer pretend her life is not coming to an end. If and when that person is ready, she turns and faces what she has been running away from.

This is the crux of mindfulness: we turn and face that which is painful, terrifying, full of grief, and we do so with kindness, with compassion, with all the self-regard and self-love we can muster. Then, as Stephen Levine attests in *A Year to Live*, his excellent work on death and dying, everything changes. The secondary suffering melts away.

So whether you're feeling the international crisis, or whether the earthquake is more in the day-to-day events of your life, know the difference between primary and secondary suffering. Name that over which you have no control. Then name that over which you do have control. It is in the second where there is hope, where your work is, where transformation will occur.

The mindfulness movement

If the escalation of global emergency is one noticeable trend, there is another too: the growth in mindfulness. At first glance they may not seem related.

Having built slowly over many decades, in the last ten years mindfulness has really caught on. It has spread through the medical community thanks to people like Jon Kabat-Zinn and his Centre for Mindfulness in Medicine, Health Care & Society, based at the University of Massachusetts Medical School. His work created a wave of research, clinical trials and practice around the world. So much so that in 2015 the Mindfulness All-party Parliamentary Group's report for the UK government, 'Mindful Nation UK', referred to the 'huge increase in academic research on the subject with more than 500 peer-reviewed scientific journal papers now being published every year' (p. 4).

This state of affairs is reminiscent of when cognitive behavioural therapy (CBT) was becoming established. Mindfulness, however, has gone far beyond the scope and reach of that particular therapy. While the 'Mindful Nation UK' report focuses on mindfulness as 'an important innovation in mental health', the practice of mindfulness has actually spread far and wide into the general population way beyond the mental health sector. It is being used as much by the well as the unwell.

Jon Kabat-Zinn, the report tells us,

> has compared mindfulness to jogging. Back in the seventies the latter was regarded as an unusual form of exercise practised by a few people; now it is recognized and promoted as an easy and effective exercise used by millions across the world with great benefits to personal health. There is a widespread consensus around the benefits of active physical exercise. (p. 6)

In other words, mindfulness is on its way to becoming established as the go-to practice for maintaining our well-being, especially our emotional and psychological well-being. Kabat-Zinn, says the report, believes that the adoption of mindfulness follows an even steeper trajectory than that of jogging.

Multinational companies such as Google, IBM and Apple now offer mindfulness to their staff, as does the British civil service. The US Marine Corps has trialled it with positive outcomes, and celebrities such as Oprah Winfrey and actress Emma Watson practise it. In the UK, the Mental Health Foundation has developed a flag-ship scheme to help disseminate mindfulness. With its emphasis on good practice and quality assurance, their Be Mindful programme is well established and well re-spected. We've also had Ruby Wax, who suffers from depression, helping to popularize mindfulness with her book and one-woman comedy show *Sane New World*.

Why the exponential growth?

The 'Mindful Nation UK' report coincided with the launch of the Sheldon Press Mindful Way series. The growth of mindfulness is, however, no coincidence. As life becomes more and more challenging, and as fear and uncertainty about the future grow, more of us are looking for a way to cope, to ease the sense of unease, the sense of dis-ease.

The systemic global crisis is encouraging us to seek new,

mindful ways of dealing with life's multiple and complex challenges. Crisis so often acts as the driver for evolution, as the catalyst for positive, transformative change. Whether we're dealing with global developments that feel beyond our control, or whether we're dealing with the immediacy of the loss of a loved one, crisis always holds this potential.

Crisis or gift?

When the family member I mentioned in the introduction phoned me out of the blue in crisis, feeling suicidal, initially I found myself in shock. It wasn't long, however, before it became apparent that this crisis was a huge gift, one that would enable her to completely turn her life around.

Every crisis is an opportunity to wake up, an opportunity to change, to heal, to grow. As Pema Chödrön says, 'When things are shaky and nothing is working, we might realize that we are on the verge of something' (*When Things Fall Apart: Heart advice for difficult times*, pp. 15–16). Reflecting on the opportunity that crisis brings, she also notes, 'The most precious opportunity presents itself when we come to the place where we think we can't handle whatever is happening. It's too much. It's gone too far' (p. 20).

When, for instance, we are suddenly sacked and asked to leave our desk the same day, all that is familiar and recognizable in our lives promptly falls away. This can happen on an inner level too, when we are going through mental breakdown or rapid psychological change and no longer recognize ourselves, no longer know who we are. We enter into a kind of chaos, into a void. We are between worlds, between the world we knew and the one to come, the one we don't yet know.

Chaos can however be regarded as positive – as space for the new, rather than a void. May we all learn, through mindfulness, to cope with the chaos of a life crisis, to be comfortable with it and ultimately to see the opportunity for transformation and healing within it.

Transforming our lives

Practising mindfulness isn't just about adding another handy technique or tool to our 'coping with life' toolbox. Yes, it is a way of being with the chaos of crisis, a way of moving through it. Yet it is much more than that; it is a means of transforming our relationship to crisis, a means of transforming ourselves and our consciousness through the increased self-awareness that we inevitably gain. It is about transforming our lives.

Let's take a look in more detail now at exactly how mindfulness works. How does it help us cope with the chaos of crisis?

2

The present moment

Kristin Neff, psychologist and author of *Self-Compassion*, tells a wonderful story about her first ever experience, when she was about 12 years old, of being in the moment. Realizing that there is only here, and only now, she ran round the house laughing and exclaiming repeatedly in delight, 'Here! Now!' In her book, Neff lays emphasis on observing what is going on just as it is. This implies an important aspect of mindfulness: that we don't judge what is in our field of awareness in any particular moment; we simply observe it. We witness and watch what is happening as closely as we can, just as it is, without adding on to it any of our stories, our stuff or our drama. Not only do we not judge it but also, as the 'Mindful Nation UK' report puts it, we pay attention 'with an attitude of curiosity and kindness'.

To this we can add a further nuance from Vidyamala Burch, co-founder of the mindfulness training school Breathworks, that mindfulness entails 'resting more fully in the moment'. This suggests that lovely quality of mindfulness of relaxing into the moment, of letting go and simply being – even in the midst of chaos.

Another name for awareness

Mindfulness is essentially awareness. It helps us to be present with 'what is', even when that's the last thing on earth we want to do. It helps us to stop running away from the pain, to stop distracting ourselves from it, from what we don't want to have to face.

Mindfulness can be thought of as a kind of 'meta-awareness', Neff tells us. We're aware that we're aware. So rather than simply getting lost in my thoughts, in my daydreaming, I become aware that I'm lost in thought, day-dreaming. The expression itself is interesting, with the emphasis on 'lost' in thought!

Not missing life

I had an example of this only the other morning, when I went for a walk in the local woods I call 'the bluebell woods', because in the spring they are a haze of mauvy-blue. As I climbed over a stile and walked through the long grass towards the woods, my mind started turning to my day's work, to this manuscript. 'What is it that people need when they're in crisis?' I asked myself. 'What did I need?' As I started to reflect on that I began to notice the sound of the nearby stream, the gurgling water. That brought me back to the moment. I realized my thoughts had been drifting off.

While there's definitely a place for that kind of reflective thinking, my aim was to enjoy the walk, not to miss it. I needed nature nurture, and to come home refreshed ready to start my day's work. Had I not noticed that my thoughts were already jumping ahead to the manuscript I might have completely missed the walk. I might have got home and hardly been aware of the lovely countryside I'd just walked through. We can miss huge chunks of our life simply by not being present to them.

With mindfulness, as we learn to watch our thoughts, emotions and physical sensations, so we bring ourselves increasingly into the present moment. As Eckhart Tolle tells us, the present moment is the only place to be, the only place to live our lives from – especially if we don't want to miss them. It is, he asserts, 'the most precious thing there is', what he calls 'the Now'. Tolle refers to the 'compulsion to live almost exclusively through memory and anticipation'. By focusing on the past and the future in this way, we risk missing the present moment.

Our preoccupation with the past, and even more so our fear for the future, tend to be accentuated when we're in crisis. When we lose a loved one, we're pulled back in time by our memories, and the thought of the future without them stretches before us seemingly without end. In reality, all we need to get through is this moment. And this moment. And this. We do that with self-compassion.

Self-compassion

Any explanation of mindfulness needs to include kindness and compassion, most especially towards ourselves. As our self-awareness grows we start to see all the ways we are not kind to ourselves, all the ways we don't nurture ourselves or take care of ourselves. At times of crisis, self-compassion and the ability to look after oneself lovingly are all the more important. We'll hear more about this in Chapter 5.

Supporting someone in crisis

It may be that you're reading this book not because you yourself are in crisis but because somebody close to you is. I think mindfulness is essential when we are caring for someone. When I supported my family member who was in crisis and in the grip of panic, it was specifically by using the mindfulness approach that I was able to keep bringing her back into the present moment. This helped to calm her down and reduced her fear of what the future would bring.

Not only can we support the person far more effectively through our mindfulness but we can also look after ourselves far better, making sure we don't get burned out. Our increased self-awareness enables us to cope much better with the huge challenges and demands of that role.

I've already mentioned a mindfulness student of mine

who chose to join one of my courses because she was supporting a close friend dying of cancer. She came on the course both for herself and for her friend. It helped her to be present with and cope with her own rollercoaster of emotions, and it enabled her to support her friend on her rollercoaster too.

This is Tina's account of how her mindfulness practice helped her cope when caring for her father.

Tina's story

I've been practising mindfulness for many years and it has helped change my relationship to things, people and events, bringing me greater serenity and calm. Of the many instances I could name, because of its power and depth, I like to remember the time around my father's death.

My father was seriously ill and I cared for him for years. At times his suffering and despair was such that I felt overwhelmed. In those moments it was difficult to find meaning in so much pain, and my sense of powerlessness gave rise to frustration and anger. I didn't know how to ease his suffering, how to calm him.

Then, I would hold his hand and sit quietly by the side of his bed, trying to synchronize my breathing with his. I would listen to the sensations in my body, the emotions passing through me, the thoughts . . . a smile, a memory, listening in silence to my sense of helplessness in the face of his suffering, somehow would transform things . . .

When he died, my perception of reality changed. Colours, shapes, smells. Everything was the same as before, but nothing would be as before. Suddenly, I felt an emptiness behind me, void of protection. Yet he had long been too weak to be able to protect me . . .

This was the first time, I think, that I fully experienced the concept of impermanence. The image that conveyed my state of being was that of a glass splintered into a thousand pieces . . . it was impossible to turn back. The pain was tearing me apart, but I didn't stand in its way, I didn't deny it, I didn't distract myself. With the breath, I entered into this pain, I got to know it, moment by moment, I cried, I explored it. In the darkest dark, one day I found a glint of light: a pure joy, deep and inexplicable but spreading outwards. My father was there, with me, for ever. Incredulous, I simultaneously felt immense pain and a timeless, causeless happiness.

In Part 2 we will look in much more detail at how to apply mindfulness in practice, including how to cope with overwhelming emotions in the way that Tina was able to. As we outline the various aspects that are helpful for dealing with crisis, there will be specific practices and exercises for you. Before we turn to that, however, let's consider the evidence base. What does research show when it comes to the effectiveness of mindfulness?

3

The research evidence

As we've seen, there has been a considerable amount of research into mindfulness, with more than 500 papers published in journals each year. At the same time, 'developments in neuroscience and psychology are illuminating the mechanisms of mindfulness', according to the 'Mindful Nation UK' report. In particular, it has been shown that mindfulness-based interventions change the physiology of the brain for the better.

The following is what the Mental Health Foundation's website has to say on the outcomes of studies into the neuroscience of mindfulness:

> Mindfulness meditation has been shown to affect how the brain works and even its structure. People undertaking mindfulness training have shown increased activity in the area of the brain associated with positive emotion – the pre-frontal cortex – which is generally less active in people who are depressed.
>
> More than 100 studies have shown changes in brain wave activity during meditation and researchers have found that areas of the brain linked to emotional regulation are larger in people who have meditated regularly for five years.

This is a reference to the relatively recent discovery that the brain can, indeed does, change and develop throughout our lives. This phenomenon, known as the neuroplasticity of the brain, represents a revolution in science. It means that through meditation we can rewire our neural pathways to bring relief from suffering. We can use the mind to change the brain. Where meditators have known for centuries, if not millennia, that meditation 'works', we now have a scientific understanding of why and how it works physiologically.

Rick Hanson, with his book *Buddha's Brain*, was one of the first to bring these ideas to popular awareness. Many have now picked up on them and written about them too, including authors such as psychotherapist Linda Graham in her book *Bouncing Back*.

Depression: preventing relapse

The 'Mindful Nation UK' report tells us that 'The strongest evidence for MBIs [mindfulness-based interventions] is in the prevention of recurrent depression'. The report also highlights how prevalent subsequent episodes can be after an initial period of depression: 'the rate of recurrence is high – following one episode of depression 50% of people will go on to have a second episode, and 80% of these will go on to have three or more episodes' (p. 20)

The evidence indicates that Mindfulness-Based Cognitive Therapy (MBCT) reduces the risk of relapse for people who experience recurrent depression on average by 43 per cent. This figure is based not on one study, but on a meta-analysis, a summary of the research findings of six different studies. Each of these was a randomized controlled trial, considered to be the most reliable kind of research, where control groups who didn't follow mindfulness courses were used as a neutral comparison. That mindfulness can reduce the risk of relapse by almost half among those struggling with depression is a significant finding, because those prone to depression are at a higher risk from suicide.

If you're in the grip of depression, helpful resources include a referral from your doctor for an MBCT course and Cheryl Rezek's book *Anxiety and Depression*, also in the Mindful Way series. In cases of greater emergency, Samaritans' helpline is available 24 hours a day, and the Maytree Sanctuary in London offers two to three nights' free accommodation and support for those feeling suicidal (see 'Useful addresses and resources' for details). Reaching out for help when you're feeling desperate isn't always easy. Even just acknowledging to yourself that you are feeling that way is a start and maybe your first step could be to tell someone how difficult you're finding it to ask for support.

If what you're struggling with is more psychospiritual in nature you can email the Spiritual Crisis Network. This is a charitable organization I set up in 2004 and is run on a voluntary basis by a combined team of those who have been through psychospiritual crisis and mental health professionals. You might also find my first book, *In Case of Spiritual Emergency*, helpful.

On the subject of books, while most of the research carried out to date has been on face-to-face mindfulness courses, the 'Mindful Nation UK' report informs us that 'there is evidence from a recent meta-analysis that self-help mindfulness-based resources such as books and online courses also lead to lower levels of depression and anxiety' (p. 20).

Self-harming

Of all the therapies suggesting the powerful, effective use of mindfulness for coping with crisis, perhaps the most convincing is Dialectical Behaviour Therapy (DBT). It was developed by Dr Marsha Linehan to help alleviate the suffering of some of the most distressed clients known to mental health services, individuals who are frequently driven to self-harming or cutting themselves and whose rates of suicide and attempted suicide are high. If you've found yourself in A&E again as a result of your self-harming, do ask your doctor or psychiatrist whether DBT is available in your area.

DBT has mindfulness at its very core. In the early stages of developing it, Linehan realized that a crucial element of the therapy was 'radical acceptance' of how life is. Linehan also realized that she herself would have to truly learn and embody radical acceptance if she were to be able to help her clients. She took herself off to a monastic community that practised mindfulness. Her time there was formative and transformative.

Research on DBT has moved on from demonstrating its effectiveness. The focus now is on trying to demonstrate *how* DBT works, exploring the processes by which therapeutic change occurs (see, for instance, Linehan's paper 'Mechanisms of change in dialectical behavior therapy: theoretical and empirical observations', 2006).

Stress less

The Mental Health Foundation reports that the research evidence for another very well-established therapy, Mindfulness-Based Stress Reduction (MBSR), shows 'a 58% reduction in anxiety levels and 40% reduction in stress.' MBSR has been the subject of research studies since the 1970s. (For more detail see the section 'The role of mindfulness in health' in the Mindfulness All-Party Parliamentary Group's report 'Mindful Nation UK', pp. 19–26.)

Living with cancer

One of the most important areas of research has been MBIs [mindfulness-based interventions] and the treatment of long-term physical health conditions . . . In terms of specific health conditions, the strongest evidence presented is for the psychological impact of living with cancer, where 43 studies including nine randomized controlled trials are described.

('Mindful Nation UK', p. 20)

This data is brought alive by Anu Gautam's experience ('Mindful Nation UK', p. 26) of how mindfulness is helping her cope with cancer.

Anu's story

I was a dynamic 26-year-old high achiever when I was diagnosed with advanced stage Hodgkin's lymphoma. I never imagined this would happen to me. My health deteriorated and I underwent several years of intensive treatment. It was hard to cope with the physical impact. But I also lost my independence and ability to function, and I felt angry and desperate.

Once the treatment was completed I tried to get back to what I'd been doing, but health problems kept getting in the way. The Breathworks mindfulness course showed me how mindfulness applied to the difficulties I was facing. The caring environment was important and so was the inspiration of the teacher, who had really embraced her own health situation.

I learned to get a distance from my thoughts and see that they weren't necessarily true. That had a massive impact. I also saw I didn't have to be pushed around by the ups and downs of illness. I started to experience a kind of peace that was always accessible, whatever was going on.

A couple of years later I was asked to choose between a bone marrow transplant that could end my life, or having just a few years without it. It was the hardest decision of my life. After the treatment I spent six weeks in isolation knowing my life might be ending, but I just stayed with what was going on, including the prospect of dying. It was an amazing time.

My cancer came back last year. That was upsetting but I knew that it was OK to be upset. I still can't lead a very active life, but my priorities have changed. The most important thing for me is continuing this journey. I feel happier and more whole each day. And it's great.

Soldiers returning from war zones

Some of the most rewarding mindfulness training I've done has been with soldiers returning from Iraq and Afghanistan. These are men and women struggling with physical health conditions and pain alongside post-traumatic stress disorder (PTSD), insomnia, depression, panic attacks and more.

Here too the initial research evidence is encouraging. The challenge with PTSD is the tendency to suppress and want to avoid painful memories and emotions. This is thought to contribute to the symptoms of PTSD. Mindfulness, instead, encourages us to acknowledge and pay attention, in a non-judgemental way, to the very memories and emotions which are so painful.

In this way, mindfulness practice provides exposure to the thoughts and physical sensations we fear. Rather than denying or trying to change those thoughts and sensations, the focus is on changing our relationship to them. We will look at this principle of stepping towards the painful, and explore some ways to practise it, in Chapter 7.

The following findings are from a pilot study by Anthony King (2013) of group Mindfulness-Based Cognitive Therapy for combat veterans with PTSD: 'The MBCT group showed significant reduction in PTSD symptoms pre- vs post MBCT . . . and 73% of patients in MBCT (compared to 33% in TAU [treatment as usual] groups) showed clinically meaningful improvement.'

Addiction recovery

Those struggling with addiction can also find themselves lurching from crisis to crisis. Mindfulness-Based Addiction Recovery (MBAR) and Mindfulness-Based Relapse Prevention (MBRP) are two therapies that have been developed in this field. Here too research has shown the efficacy of mindfulness and the use of these mindfulness-based therapeutic approaches is set to become more and more widespread.

My book *Alcohol Recovery* goes into much more detail. It includes specific practices to help with recovery and relapse prevention as well as the personal life stories of those who have successfully used mindfulness to overcome addiction.

Personal experience

Despite the 'more than 500 peer-reviewed scientific journal papers now being published every year' there is nothing like our own personal experience to prove the value of mindfulness. Not only has it helped me through two periods of profound personal crisis, but I've also seen the innumerable benefits, time and again, in the anonymous feedback forms my mindfulness students complete. They attest to how very valuable they find mindfulness and how much they get from their practice.

In Part 2 there are many different practices and exercises

for you to have a go at. Try them out. Conduct your own evidence-based research! You only need to trust *your* personal experience. Your experiential 'aha' moment is worth all the research papers put together.

Part 2

The mindfulness practices

Introduction

Kristin Neff's wonderful story about running around the house gleefully shouting 'Here! Now!' is relevant for us. It tells how she understood for the first time what mindfulness means at the experiential, visceral level, as opposed to the purely intellectual. It highlights an important fact: that mindfulness does indeed need to be learned and understood by experience. In the following chapters you'll find practices and exercises to help you experience mindfulness.

I highly recommend listening to audio recordings whenever possible, as it's best to be guided through the practices. You'll see that I've mentioned where recordings are available through my website, <www.catherine-g-lucas.com>. Once the worst of the crisis has eased, finding a class to attend is also a very good idea.

Being in the midst of chaos or crisis is not the easiest time to learn formal meditation. Yet mindfulness itself can still be hugely valuable and we can make a useful distinction between mindfulness and formal meditation. In meditation practice we usually sit on a cushion or chair for anything between 10 and 40 minutes (the Dalai Lama meditates for three or four hours early each morning!) This helps us to learn mindfulness skills, such as observing without judgement, that we can then apply throughout the day, taking the mindfulness with us through all our activities.

In times of crisis, however, if we are not already seasoned meditators, that more formal practice feels somewhat unrealistic. Even those of us who have been meditating for years or decades tend to find that in times of crisis it's most difficult to sit regularly. Our routine is likely to have gone out of the window and we may be struggling with the basics of simply keeping regular meals going and getting any sleep. For this reason I've chosen or devised short, simple mindfulness practices that feel realistic and doable, however extreme our situation.

In selecting these practices I have also kept in mind, more importantly, that if the nature of your crisis is psychospiritual, it is best to avoid formal meditation. This is because it can intensify the process of psychospiritual emergence and emergency, taking it deeper and making it go faster. What we need at such times is to slow things down and make them manageable, not speed them up. You can always come back to your practice once you're over the worst and things have settled down sufficiently. I discuss these issues, and much more, in my book *In Case of Spiritual Emergency*.

We need several things when we're in crisis; support, the ability to cope with extreme, overwhelming emotions such as fear and maybe even with severe physical pain. We need to nurture ourselves, to be as kind and gentle with ourselves as possible. Because of the intensity of crisis, we also need space around what we're experiencing. Ultimately we need to be able to surrender to the process, to allow it to unfold, to simply be.

Here in Part 2, we'll address each of these needs in turn. Each has a chapter and specific practices dedicated to it. I also use the different practices to illustrate the various principles of mindfulness. These may be new to you, or may serve as a useful revision or refresher.

Allow me to take your hand and lead you through the practices. I've experienced periods of intense, profound crisis and come through to transform my life for the better. I know that with the help of mindfulness and the right support, you can too.

4

Moment-by-moment awareness

Moment-by-moment awareness, whether of our thoughts, emotions or bodies, is the basic building block of mindfulness, of getting started. For your very first taste of moment-by-moment awareness, have a go at this Kiwi Kickstarter practice. I've devised it inspired by the classic raisin exercise used at the beginning of Mindfulness-Based Stress Reduction courses. It's intended to be light-hearted; when we're in crisis we can get bogged down and take ourselves somewhat seriously. The practice here is transcribed from my free audio recording (available through my website). You'll need, of course, a kiwi fruit!

Kiwi Kickstarter

This is a great practice to do in the morning. If you have fruit for breakfast, then you can start your day with a little mindfulness practice which will help you be more mindful for the rest of the day. You can do it with any fruit. It doesn't need to be a kiwi, just something with a bit of zing.

The practice

If you haven't got your kiwi, now is the time to fetch it. You'll need a plate, a knife, maybe a bit of kitchen paper. What I would like you to do, first, is simply look at the kiwi. It's on the plate in front of you; we're not going to touch it yet, we're simply going to look, so we're bringing in one of the senses, the sense of sight.

Look at it as if you had never seen a kiwi before. If you think about young children, at some point they will see their first ever kiwi. So it's this kind of round, furry ball, and we can see a sort of texture on the skin. Then, in your own time, pick it up. Start feeling that texture; we're bringing in a second sense now, the sense of touch.

If you let your fingertips hover over the skin, you can feel tiny hairs. Notice how sensitive the skin on your fingertips is, and really have a good old stroke of this kiwi, really be in the moment with this wonderful, furry texture.

Then – I'm going to try not to get the giggles at this point – we're going to stroke our cheek. I'd like you to just gently stroke your cheek with the kiwi . . .

It's rather delightful! Notice how the skin of your cheek is different, has a different sensitivity from the tips of your fingers.

OK, at this point we're ready to cut into the kiwi. Slice through the middle, so you're cutting it into two halves and you've got a cross section, an exquisite pattern that is unique to the kiwi in front of you. You've got the white heart of the fruit, the little black seeds dotted around, and then the markings radiating out; not forgetting, of course, the brilliant green, which is kind of . . . kiwi green. Very vivid!

We can see just from one cut through the middle that the inside has a different texture – it's much juicier, much more slippery than the skin.

What we're doing here is slowing things down. By doing so we're heightening our awareness, heightening our attention to the moment, to what's happening, and we're using our senses to do that. This is the basis of mindfulness; it's really that simple. Use the body and the senses to come into the present moment.

Now prepare yourself a piece of kiwi. Just peel a chunk, or a slice . . . now, I'm not going to do this, because I tried earlier and discovered that I couldn't speak with a piece of kiwi in my mouth . . . but when you have your piece ready, just place it on your tongue, that's all for now. Of course now we are bringing in another sense, the sense of taste, but we are also noticing that at this point it actually doesn't have a huge amount of flavour.

Then very gently, slowly, the slower the better, push your tongue up against the roof of your mouth so that the kiwi starts to dissolve, to quite literally melt in your mouth. You'll probably notice a flood of flavours; all those flavours that are released. Just be with those, luxuriating in the kiwi experience.

When you're ready, chew slowly and gently, maybe noticing the movement in your jaw, your mouth, your lips, and then swallow that piece of kiwi.

You might like to repeat this with a second or third piece. Notice how the experience is a little different every time. Maybe the flavours don't seem quite the same each time.

That's it! It's as simple as that! Mindfulness is really simple; we bring ourselves into the present moment through the senses and through the body.

Breathing with awareness

Next let's turn to the breath. In the world of meditation and mindfulness there's a great deal of emphasis on the breath. There are many good reasons for this. At the most prosaic level, it is something that is always readily available to us wherever we are and whatever we're doing. At a more symbolic level, there is something profound about the breath of life. When we're born, we take our first breath, and when we pass over, we take our last. Breath and life are one and the same.

When we're stressed, our breathing is invariably affected. In fact some of us who are experiencing prolonged stress develop chronic breath 'holding' patterns. Our central nervous system controls functions such as breathing, heart rate and digestion, whereas the sympathetic nervous system creates the body's response to stress and activates the fight or flight response. Breathing and heart rate speed up; digestion slows or stops. After the sympathetic nervous system has done its job of preparing the body for action, to get through the real or perceived emergency, another part of the nervous system known as the parasympathetic then steps in to restore normal functioning. Where stress is continual or prolonged, as it may well be during a period of crisis, the parasympathetic system will not naturally or automatically be able to step in.

Conscious, mindful breathing helps by reducing the activity of the sympathetic nervous system and by supporting the parasympathetic system. Even just a few breaths taken with awareness can help slow our heart rate and calm us down.

Melli O'Brien (aka Mrs Mindfulness) created the 2015 online Mindfulness Summit. When she experienced a harrowing family crisis she found several simple ways in which her mindfulness practice came to the rescue. She shares how breathing consciously helped in her blog post 'How to use mindfulness in times of crisis' (<www.mrs-mindfulness.com>).

> **Melli's story**
> We spoke at the [mindfulness] summit, about the power of just taking a few deep, slow, conscious breaths – especially when you're stressed. Breathing just a couple of breaths this way whenever we have felt overwhelmed has been so soothing for us all.
>
> I've also been using my time in the ICU [intensive care unit] waiting room to do these mini-breath meditations, taking this time to step out of the mind and reconnect with my body and being-ness. It's so simple, but has been profoundly nourishing.
>
> I might just close my eyes and take one long slow breath, or maybe ten, if I have a minute free. One conscious breath brings me back to my self – reminds me that the world is still turning, birds are still singing and the sun is still shining through the window. There is more to this moment than just the pain, it's all alive and it's a miracle.

Mrs Mindfulness calls this simple practice 'One conscious breath'. To make it even more effective, try putting one hand on your chest and the other on your abdomen. This will help you connect more with your body. As you take a few breaths you'll be able to feel the movement in the chest and abdomen. This is how we come into the present – by dropping down into the body and noticing any physical sensations we're aware of.

Interestingly, Dialectical Behaviour Therapy includes 'pace breathing', where the breath is consciously used to bring down emotional arousal. If you're feeling emotionally overwhelmed, dropping down into the body to feel the sensations of the breath as it moves through you will definitely help.

Holding On

When it feels like the rug has been pulled out from under your feet, when it feels as if everything known and secure is falling away, as if there's nothing to hold on to, here's a practice to help you keep hold of something very tangible, very concrete.

When I was in crisis, when my whole world was falling apart, my therapist lent me a large, round stone, something solid and real that I could hold in my hand. At night, I kept it right by my bed. When my sleep was severely disrupted by all the anxiety, I would pick it up and feel its weightiness, its solidity. It was, literally, the only thing I had to hold on to. It came, of course, with the added benefit of representing my therapist's support, his care and concern for me.

In mindfulness circles there's a great deal of talk about letting go. Although, yes, we do need to let go, we need to be able to surrender, there are also times when we need a thread to be able to hold on to, to help keep us in this level of reality, in this realm.

The practice

Go round your home and choose a reasonably weighty object, something you can hold in one hand and that has a certain tactile appeal. I have a large stone I use as a doorstop; it's heavy and quite smooth. If you can find an object which also holds some kind of positive association for you, even better. You can then bring in stronger elements of self-care and self-nurture, as this mindfulness practice will bring comfort too. Once you've chosen your object, sit down and settle somewhere.

Spend a few minutes coming back to yourself and your centre, with your object resting in front of you. Feel your sitting bones on the seat of the chair; feel your weight sinking into the chair; feel your feet connecting with the floor, the ground beneath you.

Take your awareness to the breath and follow a few cycles of the breath. Notice the rise and fall of the shoulders as you breathe in, breathe out. Notice the expansion and release of the upper torso . . . the rib cage . . . the lungs. Notice the movement in the belly. As you follow the breath notice any movement, any sensations in the body. Allow the face to be soft, the jaw, the belly, the hands resting in your lap. Allow any tension to drain away towards the earth. Let the earth take it, absorb it. You don't need to hold on to that any longer.

When you're ready, take your attention to the object. Spend a few moments, as long as you want, familiarizing yourself with it – looking at its shape, colours, contours. Again, when you feel ready – you don't want to rush this – pick it up and take the measure of its weight. You can bounce it in your hand. Feel how solid, how concrete it is. Run your fingers and thumb over its surface. Feel the texture. All we're doing is noticing how the object is. If any thoughts or judgements come up, gently allow them to flow past, and come back to the object and the objective reality of how it is right now.

Here we're using sight and touch, possibly smell too, depending on what object you chose, to bring ourselves fully into the present moment. If what you chose is comforting or reassuring in some way, you can come back to it at any time during the day and spend a few minutes picking it up, feeling its weight, looking at it. Any time you find the mind spiralling off into chaos or catastrophe you can bring it back to this solid piece of reality.

Journaling

In times of crisis there can be an awful lot of 'stuff' going round in our heads – all the dread, the catastrophizing, the trying to work it all out. It keeps our anxiety levels high, it keeps us awake at night. As well as using mindfulness to help calm the mind, it can be a huge help to simply get some of that 'stuff' out of our heads and down on paper.

This is where journaling comes in. At the best of times, a great deal of insight can come from keeping a journal on how we're getting on with the mindfulness practices. In times of crisis, it can make the difference between a wakeful night and a restful night. You can keep pen and notebook by the bed, like I did.

Now, for instance, would be a good time to start, to jot down a few notes about how you found the Holding On practice or any of the practices. There is also a lovely book by Philip Cowell, *Keeping a Journal*, that makes for a supportive resource.

Reaching out for support

As we start to get a feel for moment-by-moment awareness, we start to notice what's happening a little more, even if it's just being aware that our heart is racing and we need to spend a minute or two consciously breathing.

Reaching out for support is a fundamental need when in crisis. My hope is that as you start to notice what's happening, you'll start to become aware of your patterns around asking for help. Are you someone who finds it difficult or easy? Do you tend to leave it a bit too late? Are there some kinds of help that are easier to ask for than others?

Using books and online resources to help with mindfulness practice is great, but in terms of our need for support they can leave us isolated and alone with our struggles. As you journal, spend time reflecting on support. What support do you have? What more might be helpful right now? If you find asking for help tricky, is there someone you can talk this through with?

The focus of our next chapter is another vital aspect of coping with crisis, one that is central to mindfulness: self-compassion. As our self-awareness and self-compassion grow, so too does our ability to reach out for support.

5

Self-compassion

Kristin Neff has written about her shock and grief on discovering her son was autistic. In her book *Self-Compassion*, she also describes how embracing her pain helped her connect with the pain of others. Connecting with others meant she felt less isolated in her pain, and able to feel the joy, love and wonder of parenting too.

Embracing is precisely what we need to do. We can embrace our pain; we can embrace ourselves.

The Selfie Hug

I've devised the 'Selfie Hug', inspired by Kristen Neff. This transcript of my recording is available as a free audio at <www.insighttimer.com> and is proving to be very popular. It's been listened to thousands of times. (See 'Useful addresses and resources', under 'Audio recordings', for details.)

I've called this practice the Selfie Hug because it involves, quite literally, giving ourselves a hug. It might feel a little bit strange, a little bit silly at first, but I certainly recommend persevering with it. When we hug ourselves, we release a hormone called oxytocin, also known as the hormone of love and bonding. Research has shown that oxytocin soothes painful emotions and calms stress.

Some people take to this practice very readily. My husband, for example, absolutely loves it; at the moment, he's doing it at the end of his meditation practice every morning. I haven't found it quite as easy, though, quite as natural, as he seems to. If that's the case for you too, be kind to yourself. Be gentle with it, explore what any resistance might be about. So let's have a go right now, let's dive straight in there.

The practice

If you're sitting down, take a moment to sense into your body . . . How is it feeling right now? Notice your contact with the ground, through your feet . . . through the seat of the chair, and notice your breath . . . What is the quality of your breathing like right now?

Then, when you are ready, in your own time, we are going to wrap our arms around our upper body and give ourselves a hug . . . mmmmm! Squeeze as tightly as you want – don't worry, you won't break any ribs! Spend as long as you want with your arms wrapped around yourself – maybe even gently rocking, soothing yourself. You can stroke your arms, if you want; give your arms a nice stroke, or even your face . . . Mmmmm! . . . that feels particularly lovely, that skin-on-skin contact. I suspect that it releases even more oxytocin. Then, when you are ready, just let your arms drop back down again.

When you're first getting used to this practice, I recommend you do it several times a day for the first couple of weeks. That way, when you really need it, when you are struggling with something, it will be that much easier.

If you notice any resistance, and that may be for all sorts of reasons (do you find it a bit difficult to be kind to yourself sometimes?), try journaling to explore what is going on. The beauty of this practice, of course, is you can do it anywhere, any time; if you are in public, and you want to be discreet, you can just casually fold your arms and give yourself a little squeeze. What could be simpler? So, give it a go; see how you get on with it . . .

What we're doing here is cultivating a sense of caring towards ourselves, a sense that we are precious and worthy of our love, that we want to do our best to take care of ourselves. Every time you give yourself a hug or a tender stroke of the cheek or arm, you'll be strengthening your self-compassion muscles!

As well as embracing ourselves and embracing our suffering, we can also embrace each other. If you've got family or friends around, and especially if you're not the only one feeling distressed, try a group hug.

Breathing together

I remember some dear friends recently sharing some very painful news with my husband and me. After we had spent some time around the table, holding hands together, listening, sharing, talking, crying, talking some more, when things came to a natural close, we all instinctively stood up, and the four of us had a group hug and simply breathed together. So I can recommend this from personal experience.

Breeze Bathing

Mrs Mindfulness encourages us to do things that nourish us during challenging times. I couldn't agree more. Some of the practices I've developed feel particularly appropriate for nurturing ourselves, for giving ourselves the chance to simply be with what is. Once we've had that all-important 'aha' insight when we cotton on to the fact that this is in reality a moment of suffering, we can tenderly give ourselves the opportunity to explore it, rather than running away from it. We can show ourselves compassion.

'Breeze Bathing' speaks to me of self-nurture and self-care – and it's safer than sun-bathing! This is a seasonal practice in that you'll need to be outside, at a time of year when it's warm enough, with a gentle breeze. This practice is transcribed from my audio recording, which is available free at <www.catherine-g-lucas.com>.

The practice

I think it's fair to say that this is a spring or summer practice, maybe an autumn one; it's not really suitable for winter because you don't want a gale force wind blowing for this practice. A nice gentle breeze is ideal. You're going to want to be outside somewhere; I'm actually lying on a bench with a long cushion underneath me.

Get yourself comfortable, preferably lying down, but you don't have to be – and then make sure you have some skin that is bare so that you can feel the breeze on your skin. It could be just your face, but actually today is a lovely sunny, warm day, so I've got my arms and legs exposed.

So let's just take a moment to arrive; letting go of whatever activities we've been doing, any busyness of the day, just breathing in and breathing out . . . giving ourselves permission to be fully here . . . in this moment . . . in this place.

You can feel your weight sinking down, especially if you are lying down. Let go of your weight and feel the connection with the ground, with the earth beneath you, the whole planet, the whole earth, supporting you in this moment.

Then, whether you are sitting or lying, notice the points of contact between you and the surface, the ground, whatever you are lying or sitting on; maybe notice the back of your head . . . the back of your shoulders . . . the length of your back . . . your buttocks.

If you are sitting, maybe particularly notice your sitting bones . . . and then maybe the backs of your legs, or if you have your knees bent up like I have, then particularly feel the soles of your feet . . . bare feet is rather lovely, if it's warm enough for you. Just notice the surface, the texture underneath your bare feet.

Then let's follow the breath, follow the movements and sensations of the breath, through the body for a few moments . . . breathe in, feeling the rise of the belly . . . breathe out, feeling the belly subsiding . . . maybe noticing the movement in your upper torso as well . . .

The lungs filling . . . the chest expanding, and then the lungs emptying and the chest releasing. Then follow a few cycles of the breath . . . noticing all those sensations, all the movements, the myriad movements . . .

Then, in your own time, turn your attention to skin, to your bare skin . . . really home in on one particular part of your body where you have bare skin . . . noticing any sensations there; maybe the warmth of the sun . . . just starting to notice the breeze.

If it's quite a gentle breeze, these are going to be very delicate sensations . . . and depending on how frequently the breeze is blowing, this is going to be a practice of watching and waiting, a practice of being receptive, and when the breeze comes, feeling it ripple over your skin . . . ripple along your body . . . and the breeze comes and goes, very much like our thoughts, like our feelings, we just allow them to come . . . and let them go.

This is very much about being receptive; just allowing the breeze to come, and then, when it does, just allowing it to pass. Noticing how delicate the sensations are; or sometimes, if the breeze comes in a little flurry, that the sensations are a bit stronger, maybe a bit cooler . . . and all the while, the body is breathing itself . . . we have these undulations, these waves of the breath moving through the body, like the breeze moving across the skin.

Notice the movement of the breeze. It kind of moves around the skin in little eddies, in little flurries; it's not one clean brushstroke, it's more of a dance, a delicious dance . . .

So we are just being with the breeze, breathing with the breeze . . . and really giving ourselves the time and space to notice these delicate sensations, and just how delicious they can be when we give ourselves the time, and the space.

Notice the change in temperature with each little flurry and surrender your whole being to the breeze. There is nothing that you need to do right now, nowhere you need to go.

You can carry this practice on for as long as you want.

When you're ready, you can start gently wrapping up, becoming more aware of your surroundings . . . opening your eyes, if you have them closed . . . maybe having a little bit of a stretch . . .

I hope you've enjoyed this practice today. It's one you can come back to again and again.

The Ultimate Bath Experience

If you're looking for a nurturing practice and the weather isn't warm enough to be outside for Breeze Bathing, then I suggest the Ultimate Bath Experience.

The practice

The Ultimate Bath Experience involves appealing to as many senses as possible. Putting some aromatherapy oils in the water will give you a lovely scent. Lavender, for instance, is very relaxing. If you add some extra, neutral oil, the wonderful feeling on your skin will bring in the sense of touch.

Treat yourself to little snacks such as fruit; something like the kiwi we used for the Kiwi Kickstarter, or maybe raspberries or mango. This brings in the sense of taste . . . choose your favourite.

Ideally have a bath cushion for extra pampering. Candles or tea-lights add to the relaxing ambience too. Go for the full works!

Then, to bring in even more great mindfulness practice, you can listen to a recording of a Body Scan and do the practice lying in the bath. The Body Scan is the classic body awareness practice. It usually lasts somewhere between 20 and 40 minutes and there are many free versions available on the web, including on my website. Enjoy!

I have to confess, The Ultimate Bath Experience is my go-to stressbuster. Since reading Kristin Neff's book *Self-Compassion*, I've become much more aware of moments of suffering, however great or small, and when I need to be kind to myself.

Kindness towards ourselves when times are tough is non-negotiable. It can indeed be painful when the bottom falls out of our lives and there's nothing familiar left to hang on to. The pain we're dealing with may be emotional or psychological, of the heart or of the mind, but equally it may be of the body. Writing about coping with physical pain in *A Year to Live*, Stephen Levine encourages us to send loving kindness to whichever part of the body is hurting, without embarrassment. In Chapter 7 we will explore more fully how to cope with physical pain.

Kindfulness retreats

As we've seen, so much of mindfulness is actually kindness, being compassionate towards our own suffering. To help you cultivate that, you can listen to my Loving Kindness audio through my website. There are also many other free versions available on the web.

Self-compassion is inherent in mindfulness. When we learn and practise mindfulness, our self-compassion and self-nurture inevitably grow. I remember one particular Living Well with Stress course I was teaching, during which quite early on, in only about the second session, the whole group suddenly realized that it was all about self-care. It was a group lightbulb moment!

As kindness is so central to our practice, among the retreats I run is a one-day Kindfulness retreat. The retreats serve as both a useful introduction to mindfulness and compassion for anyone new to it and, for more seasoned meditators, as an opportunity to spend a day practising. For details see my website.

In this chapter we've touched on that mindfulness classic, the Body Scan. In the next, we'll go into more depth about how and why the body is so central to our practice. We'll look at how in crisis or in chaos it can be our refuge, our place of comfort, our saviour.

6

Being in our bodies

In times of crisis, often the last place we want to be, the last place we're to be found, is in our bodies. We spiral off into catastrophic thinking and drown in emotional overwhelm. This is why mindfulness therapies such as Mindfulness-Based Cognitive Therapy have been so successful; they get us out of our heads and into our bodies. If you're in a great deal of physical pain, that may not seem very appealing, but in the next chapter we will see just how much sense it makes, in fact, and how to work with that pain.

The Body Scan

As I've mentioned, it is through the body and its senses that we come into the present. I hope you had an experience of this when you tried the Kiwi Kickstarter. Do you remember, when I was walking through the bluebell woods, that it was the sound of water, the sense of hearing, that brought me back to the moment, that helped me notice my wandering, wondering mind? This is why, when we're in crisis and need to be able to get through just this moment, it is the body we need to return to. This is not something we do once, but over and over again. As Matthew Sandford, who was paralysed from the waist down at the age of 13, says, 'I am still returning to my body and will do so for the rest of my life.' Matthew was involved in a severe car accident. Years later he discovered yoga. Rather than turn away from his body, he turned towards it. Today he is a yoga teacher and an inspiration to many.

The best mindfulness practice for returning to our bodies is the Body Scan. It is *the* classic mindfulness practice, the one that defines mindfulness programmes more than any other. By doing the Body Scan virtually every day for the six- or eight-week duration of a mindfulness course, we find that by the end of it we have transformed our relationship with our body. We can no longer forget it or simply ignore it. We can no longer treat it harshly or ride roughshod over its needs. Instead we notice it, care for it and take care of it.

You'll need to download an audio version of the Body Scan for this practice. There are many free versions available on the web, including through my website. The various versions last anywhere from 10 to 40 minutes, and the longer ones go into more detail. On the whole, the more often you listen, and the longer the version, the more benefit you'll gain. The version on my website is about 25 minutes long.

The practice

We do the Body Scan lying down, on the sofa, on the bed, on the grass. We support the head with a pillow or cushion, making sure it's not too high so that the neck doesn't feel strained in any way. We rest the arms either by our sides or with the hands lying gently on the belly, whichever feels more natural and comfortable. We have some sort of blanket or throw over us, as the body temperature invariably drops while we're doing the Body Scan. Then we listen to a recording of someone talking us through the Body Scan, guiding us to take our attention to each part of the body in turn. Usually the Body Scan starts at the head and works its way down to the feet, or vice versa.

I remember when I was supporting a dear friend through crisis, she would lie on the sofa and I would lie on the rug in front of the stove. Rumi, her cat, would join us and I'd talk all three of us through the Body Scan. It's a particularly lovely practice in challenging times because, while being a body awareness practice, it has the added benefit of being very relaxing. Relaxing and softening is very much what we need in the midst of life's challenges.

Getting extra support

When I first started studying with Breathworks to become a mindfulness trainer, I discovered that I had spent years meditating in my head, rather than in my body. Like many of us in the West, I was living in my head, not in my body. For some of us our relationship with our body is further complicated by an experience or history of sexual violation. If this is the case for you, then consciously – or unconsciously – you may well not feel completely comfortable with your body, with inhabiting it fully. This is totally understandable.

The practice that helped me make friends with my body was the Body Scan. However, in one mindfulness study carried out among war veterans, those who had experienced some sort of sexual assault struggled with the Body Scan. If you are carrying sexual wounding of some kind, you may well need extra help from a counsellor or therapist to be able to engage with body practices such as the Body Scan or mindful movement. Ultimately this can be a deeply healing journey for you so do give it careful consideration – it might help.

Likewise, if your relationship with your body is such that in order to gain relief from unbearable emotional pain you self-harm in some way, such as by self-cutting, then a therapy such as Dialectical Behaviour Therapy could help enormously. The national charity Self Injury Support has a range of resources for young people who self-harm, including *The Rainbow Journal* (see 'Useful addresses and resources'). I produced this in collaboration with a group of youngsters while working for the charity.

Mindful movement

So far we've covered the Body Scan. The other component of mindfulness training that focuses explicitly on the body is mindful movement. Yoga is an integral component of many mindfulness programmes and was built into Jon Kabat-Zinn's original Mindfulness-Based Stress Reduction course; some programmes, such as Living Well with Pain and Illness, offered by Breathworks, include gentle mindful movement exercises as an alternative. These are better suited to those with injuries, pain or illness. Core Process Psychotherapy, which is mindfulness-based, uses an even more gentle mindful movement, one which is carried out very slowly indeed.

All these practices help us build our mindfulness muscles. They help us connect more effectively with the body and they help us learn to be mindful in movement as well as in rest. Perhaps more importantly, they assist us in exploring our patterns around holding and resisting. Where do we tense up in the body? Where are we holding in our lives? Connecting with the body, whether through yoga, mindful movement or the Body Scan, aids us in loosening and softening.

Mindful Walking

If you're physically well enough, I suggest walking mindfulness practice as one of the simplest forms of mindful movement. The beauty is we can do it virtually anywhere, any time. I even remember, when I was in Egypt, going through psychospiritual crisis, walking up and down the long hallway of a hotel in the middle of the night.

The following is transcribed from my audio recording, available through my website. If you're walking on grass or sand, doing so barefoot is delicious!

The practice

Today we are going to take a walk together. Do join me; I'm actually on the south coast, at a place called Highcliffe, in Dorset. You can probably hear the waves in the background, but you can do this walk anywhere. You can get out in nature, but equally an urban setting is fine too.

Before we start, just take a moment standing on the spot, feel your contact with the ground through your feet. Maybe bend your knees a little, flex your knees, your legs, bounce up and down a little bit just to feel your weight, your body, that contact with the earth. I hope you can hear me above the sound of the waves.

We're going to start taking a few, slow, gentle steps. As you do so, bring your attention to your feet, to the soles of your feet, and notice the motion on the ball of your foot. As you put your heel down and roll your foot forwards to the ball of your foot, and then your toes, kind of push off again. Just notice that . . . Slow your pace down so that you can really feel the separate bits of each step. Notice when one foot takes over from the other, the transition point.

Maybe notice the texture of the ground underneath. How much give is there in the earth, in the ground that you are walking on? The sand here today, on the beach, is actually quite firm. I'm quite close to the water's edge so the sand is quite wet.

Then you might like to start to notice what's happening in some of the bones, the little bones in your feet, in your toes, the muscles. Notice the movement in your ankle with each step. You can either keep your focus on your feet, the soles of your feet, or you might like to start gradually working your way further up the legs, further up the body, noticing the ankles, the movement in the ankles; noticing what is happening in the shins, the calves.

You can maybe feel your clothing against your skin. If you're walking uphill or downhill, notice the difference, how that feels different in your calf muscles. Where I am today is actually pretty flat.

Then notice the knees, the role that the knees play in each step, the point at which the leg seems to almost straighten out, and then the knees bend more with each forward step. Then come up to the thighs, big muscles, big bones in the thighs and feel those.

Then we can take our attention on up to the hips. With the hips there isn't just a movement forwards and backwards, as we walk – notice also the side-to-side motion that takes place. As you walk along at a fairly even pace, you can just get into the flow, into the swing of each step following the one before.

You might like to experiment with varying the speed, going slower, or faster – whoops, I'm just about to get wet shoes here ... ! Notice the arms as well. Notice this lovely, natural rhythm of the arms just swinging, hanging freely by your sides, swinging backwards and forwards. You can get into a really nice rhythm, following the body and following the breath; noticing what is happening with the breath as well. Sometimes in traditional walking meditation, the steps are done in sync with the breath.

You can carry on as long as you would like to, 5, 10, 15 minutes. The trick is to always bring your mind back; if your mind starts to wander off, which it naturally will do, then you just bring it back to the body, bring it back to the senses, the sensations, the movement in the body. This has the wonderful effect of bringing us into the present moment, rather than the mind dragging us here, there and everywhere. We gently bring the mind into the here and now through the body and through the movement of the body.

So, have fun with this. Try it in different environments, different places, at different speeds. I would recommend that you do it without eating, without talking, simply focusing on one step at a time.

If you're not able to walk and can only manage gentle upper-body stretches, some of the exercises developed by Breathworks can be found in Vidyamala Burch's *Living Well with Pain and Illness*.

Grounding

Becoming embodied and getting grounded are closely related to each other. The more we inhabit our bodies, the more we can connect with the ground beneath us. When it feels like the rug has been pulled out from under our feet, we need to connect with the ground beneath it. There is safety and comfort in feeling solid earth beneath us. The earth can support us, can absorb our stress, our pain, if we're willing to let it go, to let it drain away into the very soil beneath us.

During a mental health or psychospiritual crisis, lack of grounding can be a serious issue. If we are not sufficiently grounded, not sufficiently in touch with or connected with our bodies, the crisis can escalate further. The most extreme scenario is when people think they can breathe under water or fly and, as a result, seriously hurt or even kill themselves. Fortunately, this is very rare.

Here is Deborah's account of the importance of grounding and how, through her experience of mindfulness and meditation, she was able to offer her sister crucial support. (Psychospiritual crisis is also known as spiritual crisis or spiritual emergency, a term coined by psychiatrist Stanislav Grof.)

Deborah's story

I live overseas and hadn't been around to support my sister after her marriage crumbled. Other family members were doing their best to help and support her while she tried to cope with a newborn baby and a child of primary school age. However, the shock and emotional heartache, as well as the financial strain of being a single mum, took its toll. As a result she had a spiritual emergency and was admitted on to a psychiatric ward.

During the two weeks I visited my sister in hospital while she was in the throes of her crisis, I made the conscious decision to stay heart centred and present during our daily hour of visiting. Having practised meditation and mindfulness for several years, as well as having studied different energy modalities, I had an understanding of what may have brought about her crisis, which did away with any fear that other members of my family were experiencing.

I knew as soon as I saw her on the first day that she was completely ungrounded. I knew that she was completely blown open and that was why, at this stage, she was overly sensitive to every stimulus from all five senses. She had a heightened sense of smell and complained of our body odour and smelly feet, even though we had all showered beforehand.

The birds chirping outside were extremely noisy and irritating to her. We also all had to talk in a whisper. Any food or drink she was given was 'toxic', and getting her to wear clothes was a challenge as she didn't like the feeling of them against her skin. She was also 'seeing' spirits – our deceased father, grandmother and aunt.

The first thing I did was to ground her. We did some breath work together while standing, whereby I got her to imagine that with every out breath, she pushed all the excess energy out through the soles of her feet into the earth. After several rounds, when I felt she was back with us, I did some deep meditation and breathing work with my sister, asking her to imagine that she was closing herself off from undue outside stimulus. I asked her to breathe into the space in her body and imagine it closing up like a flower.

She did this daily and one by one, the oversensitivities of the senses dissipated and she became more present and alert. By the time she was discharged, two weeks later, she was fully present and all five senses were normal. She certainly seemed like her old self again.

I felt that I helped my other family members during those two weeks also; by staying centred and strong, it had a positive, helpful impact on them. Each day I did a meditation in the morning and remained heart centred.

My family couldn't believe the dramatic improvement in my sister in such a short time, and the doctor and staff were also extremely surprised and wanted to know more. I referred them to the book *In Case of Spiritual Emergency* and the Spiritual Crisis Network website.

My sister, since her discharge four months ago, has done a meditation weekend workshop and a writers' workshop, and is doing so well. She grounds herself daily, practises being present and meditates regularly. She has moved on completely and her main focus is her well-being and that of her two beautiful children.

Through her understanding of grounding and her experience of mindfulness meditation, Deborah was able to help her sister enormously. Grounding activities can be anything from pottering about in the garden to peeling vegetables, from going for a stroll to cleaning the bathroom. The important thing is to focus very much on the body, simply bringing the mind gently back when it goes walkabout. (For more on grounding and grounding practices, see my book *In Case of Spiritual Emergency*.)

Letting go of our bodies

In our relationship with our bodies there is a seeming paradox. On the one hand, it is through our bodies and our senses that we come into the present moment. Our bodies are an essential vehicle for being here, now. Yet we also need to know that we are not our bodies; in the same way that we are not our thoughts, not our feelings. These are ephemeral things that come and go. We do not want to get caught up in them. We do not want to believe them. We are so much more than them. Our bodies too are ephemeral, our bodies too come and go, although we tend to think of them as far more concrete, far more 'real' than thoughts or feelings.

So while we want to learn to keep returning to our bodies time and again, to fully inhabit them, especially in challenging situations, we also need to be able to let go of them when the time comes. It is perhaps only by fully inhabiting our bodies that we can easily transcend them at the end of our lives. Stephen Levine writes beautifully on this in *A Year to Live*. If you or a loved one have been given a terminal diagnosis I highly recommend Levine's book. He will enfold you in his arms and gently accompany you through the fear, the grief, the unknown. He will show you how to return to your body, how to love it and how to lovingly let it go.

7

Coping with physical pain

In this chapter we're going to explore a fundamental principle of mindfulness, one which feels counter-intuitive yet is at the heart of how our practice helps make pain, physical or emotional, bearable. We're going to look at opening to, gently turning towards, even stepping towards that which is painful. Our natural instinct might be to run in the opposite direction. If we do, all that will happen is that our pain will chase us down the road!

Before we look at that, I'd like to share with you journalist Danny Penman's story, in the book he wrote with Vidyamala Burch, *Mindfulness for Health*. It shows the power of mindfulness, even in the face of severe injuries and extreme pain. I saw similar results when I taught mindfulness to soldiers returning from war zones.

Danny's story

Danny had a serious paragliding accident in the Cotswolds. In desperation, he began using a form of meditation he'd learned at school, making himself breathe slowly and consciously even while still lying on the ground just after the accident. This helped him manage the excruciating pain, breath by breath. He needed three major operations to rebuild his leg. Struggling with continuing pain and lack of sleep during the recovery period, he decided to find an alternative way of coping.

Danny turned to mindfulness. He found it enormously helpful. As his pain diminished he was able to reduce the number of painkillers he took drastically. His doctors were amazed at his recovery and managed to remove the frame from his injured leg after only four months, rather than the usual six to eighteen. Since then Danny has taken up running and has hiked Britain's South West Coast Path, all 630 miles of it!

Danny's story is truly inspiring. Not only did mindfulness help him cope with the excruciating pain he experienced at the moment of the accident itself but it also helped him cope with the ongoing pain and the challenging months afterwards. Just as important, mindfulness helped him deal with the emotional impact of the injury. Major accidents and illness all too often bring anxiety, stress and depression. By coping with those as well, Danny was able to make an impressive recovery.

Plain Rain

Just how does mindfulness achieve these extraordinary results? What makes it so effective? How do we cope with, work with, be with that level of ongoing pain and discomfort? It all comes down to gently stepping towards the painful, gently leaning into it, softening into it. We've already seen that we need heartfuls of kindness and tenderness towards ourselves and our pain. We can now take ourselves by the hand and lovingly lead ourselves towards that which we would rather avoid.

Before you have a go at a practice that involves softly turning towards and exploring physical pain, I've devised something that will help you try the same principles but in a much less loaded situation. We often contract around wet weather. Nobody wants to get wet. Unless we're keen gardeners, we tend to see rain as unwelcome, as 'bad', 'not good', 'a nuisance'.

So we're going to have a go at suspending our judgements. We're going to step towards and explore that which we would normally rather avoid. You'll need an umbrella. When you first have a go at this practice, I suggest a fairly warm day of gentle rather than lashing rain. You can progress to that more advanced version later!

The practice

I'd like to invite you to come for a walk in the rain with me, under our umbrellas. Once outside, take a few moments initially to connect with your body, with your feet treading the earth, with your breath.

Feel the soles of your feet connecting with the ground, feel the rhythm of your steps, feel the rhythm of your breath.

When you're ready, turn your attention to the sound of the rain on your umbrella. As you stroll along, focus on the rhythm of the rain, its cadence. Is it steady or intermittent? Is it barely audible or quite insistent? Is it drizzling? Spitting? Showering? Stay focused on the sound, on the immediate, simple experience of the soft drumming.

If the mind goes galloping off, gently rein (sorry!) it in, come back to the pattering of the raindrops on the umbrella. You can carry on with this first part of the practice as long as you like.

When you're ready, if you're ready, you can move on to the next part. This involves taking your umbrella down and feeling the water droplets on your skin, maybe your face or your forearms. Before you close the umbrella, come back to the breath, an awareness of the breath, soften your body, your belly, soften your face, your jaw.

You are going to get wet. Can you be open to that without judging it, without resisting it? What does it feel like to be getting wet? Can you be receptive to that? Do you notice yourself recoiling at first and then relaxing into it or are you aware of your whole body contracting against it?

As with all mindfulness, there's no right or wrong, just noticing how it is for you. When you get back home, maybe jot down some of your impressions in your journal.

Softening into pain

Once you've had a chance to experiment with opening towards something you might usually avoid or resist (the rain), try to start gradually exploring your pain. Make yourself comfortable and settle down, with a throw or blanket over you. Maybe start with a Selfie Hug (see p. 47) to remind yourself of your loving concern and care for yourself. If at any point it feels too much, know that you can always come back to it later when you're feeling more resourced.

The practice

In *A Year to Live*, Stephen Levine suggests settling into the moment as it is and allowing ourselves to feel the discomfort. We are used to withdrawing our awareness from the unpleasant and hurtful – to 'armour our hearts' as Levine says. In his book, Levine invites us to allow awareness to go where it may never have been before, and to explore the resulting sensations in as calm a manner as possible. View them as a process, and see if any shape to them emerges.

I would add the following key questions to ask yourself.

♥ What else is in my experience in this moment?

♥ If I open to the pain, what else can I open to?

♥ Are there parts of the body that are not in discomfort, that feel OK or even good right now?

We tend to have ideas or beliefs about pain that are not necessarily true; that it is fixed and unchanging, for instance. This practice encourages us to explore it and dismantle some of those beliefs; to discover all the ways in which pain is ever changing, coming in ebbs and flows, in eddies and flurries. It is only by gently opening to it, by tenderly stepping towards it, that we can discover these things. We also tend to think, or even believe, that pain is the only thing in our experience right now. 'What else is in my experience in this moment?' is indeed a key question to ask yourself.

Working with the resistance

If it's seemingly as simple as gently turning towards the painful, what is it that stops us? Resistance. Resistance,

Levine says, 'turns pain into suffering, the unpleasant into the unbearable.' Our work, then, is to unmask the resistance, to name it, explore it. Here is a clue to its presence. If you find yourself thinking 'Why is this happening to me?' or 'I don't want this to be happening to me', then resistance has crept, or stormed, its way in.

Notice I say in the title above 'the' resistance rather than 'our' resistance – we are dealing with the universal nature of resistance, not something peculiar to me or to you, that only I or you struggle with. Everyone struggles with resistance. It's good to remember that when it's our turn to face it!

Resistance in times of crisis

At the best of times, resistance to life 'as it is' creeps in. We climb over one stile only to come to the next. In times of crisis, though, the resistance is more likely to feel like a brick wall than a wooden stile. In her book *Living Well with Pain and Illness*, Vidyamala Burch, the co-founder of Breathworks, tells how she hit her personal brick wall. The following story tells how the resistance for her took the shape of an inner battle through the night. As chaos gave way to clarity, the resistance melted away.

> ### Vidyamala's story
> Vidyamala had injured her spine as a teenager. In her early twenties she had a very serious car accident which damaged her spine further. A few months later she went back to work, but her spine was very painful and working was physically and emotionally very demanding for her.

After struggling on for another two years, using will power to push through, Vidyamala eventually could no longer keep going. She reached crisis point when, having been bed-bound for several months and on the neurosurgical intensive care ward, her bladder stopped functioning.

Required on doctor's orders to sit upright for 24 hours, she found the long hours of the night unbearable, until in her agony she realized that she didn't have to get through the whole night – only through the present moment. Immediately, her experience was transformed, and she relaxed into an accepting, expansive state. The realization applied not just to the present torture of being obliged to sit up through a harrowing night after a medical investigation, but also to life, which can only unfold one moment at a time.

Vidyamala's experience illustrates graphically the contrast between resistance making things unbearable and the relief once it melts away. It is also a perfect example of how, when in crisis, we only need to get through one moment at a time. This is how I supported my relative through crisis – by focusing on just getting through each moment of panic at a time.

Acceptance as the gateway to change

What Dialectical Behaviour Therapy and other mindfulness-based therapies set out to achieve is a balance between total acceptance of how things are right now and at the same time working towards change. Ironically, it is only when we can be with what is, however painful and challenging, without judging it and without the slightest resistance to it, that change can happen. It is when we resist, when we don't want our lives, our feelings, our thoughts or our bodies to be how they are, that we get stuck, that change is not possible. Much of what we learn in mindfulness is learning to spot resistance in all its cunning disguises.

'This Too'

This chapter has been about softening into physical pain, gently stepping towards it. The same principle applies equally to emotional, psychological pain. We're learning to be open, to be receptive, to allow.

The practice

Mrs Mindfulness suggests the perfect mantra to help with resistance: 'This too', or, 'This too is allowed and accepted'.

I have found this a very helpful mantra to remember, especially when combined with 'One conscious breath' (p. 42) or several breaths taken with awareness.

In times of difficulty you can simply repeat the words quietly to yourself. If you become aware of any kind of resistance, such as wanting to push away physical or emotional pain, these words can help to remind you to soften into it, to gently open to it.

Equally, if you become aware of thoughts such as 'Why is this happening to me?' or 'I don't want this to be happening', repeat the phrase softly to yourself. Make it your own; maybe 'I'm willing to accept this too' or 'I choose to allow this', or whatever works for you.

Physical pain rarely visits us alone. It often brings its companion, fear, with it. In the next chapter we'll be looking at coping with the kind of dread and terror that crisis invites in. How do we cope with emotional overwhelm?

8

Coping with overwhelming fear

Freedom from fear

Stephen Levine says there is nothing to fear in fear. But, of all the emotions we experience when in crisis, the most common and most dominating is fear. Our feelings of fear can be crippling. They can escalate and turn into panic or sheer terror. Much of this dread is about what is going to happen – or rather what we imagine is going to happen. In essence this is fear about the future, about some unformed, unshaped, undetermined outcome. Vidyamala, whose story we looked at in the last chapter, says she realized that much of her torment had grown out of her fear of the future.

Sitting with uncertainty

A less extreme version of fear of the future is the uncertainty of not knowing how things are going to turn out.

This can be just as challenging in its own way, depending on the circumstances. Writing about the global state of crisis in their book *Active Hope*, Joanna Macy and Chris Johnstone speak of 'making friends with uncertainty'.

Our practice can help us make 'friends with uncertainty' and its gifts, even if these appear unfamiliar and strange at first. We can gradually learn to sit with, to be with, the unknowing of the future, the uncertainty that lies ahead. With mindfulness we can change our relationship to that uncertainty. Chris Johnstone describes how, after a car accident, he had resigned from his job and now had no idea what he was going to do. Yet, even while his legs were like jelly with fear, it struck him that this not knowing was part of the mystery of life – a cause for excitement, not fear!

Both Vidyamala and Chris had moments of clarity, of breakthrough. These are all the more likely to come if we're able to 'stay with' the challenging situation and the emotions it brings. If we can stay with it, we can find our way through it.

Acknowledging fear

It's important to recognize and acknowledge fear. Our feelings are real and they matter. We don't want to deny them or suppress them in any way, yet we do also want to transform them. It's acceptance which can make change possible. So the first step is simply noticing, with mindful awareness, what is happening for us emotionally. This can be challenging if we are simply drowning in that fear, overwhelmed and consumed by it. The more we develop our mindfulness muscles, the more we develop the 'witness' who simply observes what is going on. Here we can use a method known as 'noting'.

Noting

'Noting' helps us learn to spot our different states of mind, our different emotions, to become more aware of them. We can then work with bringing our attention back to the body, back to the breath, feeling our connection with the ground beneath us.

The practice

At various times through the day, stop and ask yourself what is in your mind, in your heart, at this particular moment. Is it daydreaming? Worrying? Planning? Is it catastrophizing? Going over a conversation? Rehearsing one? Is it fearing? Reminiscing? Ruminating? Maybe it's loving, longing or laughing? Can you see how many of these mental states are either taking us into the future or back to the past? They are taking us away from the present.

Set some sort of a timer to go off at regular, or irregular, times during the day. You probably have one on your phone. Alternatively, use a natural prompt; maybe every time you stand up or sit down, or every time you turn a light on or off, something that will remind you to note your mental state in that moment. This is a good way of noticing what's happening as it's happening. It helps bring us into the present; it helps us become more present.

Catching fear early

The earlier we are able to 'note' fear, to catch fear, the easier it will be. When I was in crisis in Egypt and ended up in a wheelchair for a few days because my legs gave way, I saw how fear contributes enormously to heightening the sense of crisis. It also seemed that, of all the emotions, fear had the least substance. As I watched its machinations, it felt like a complete fabrication of the mind, of the ego, with no reality of its own. Nevertheless, I still had to grapple with an underlying level of anxiety for some time after the peak of the crisis and the terror had passed.

Hello Fear

The way we work with fear, and any other strong emotion, is very similar to how we work with pain. We acknowledge it, we open to it, we explore it. This is fundamental to mindfulness. In the practice I've devised we're going to say 'hello' to fear. We may not be ready to welcome fear with open arms, but at least we can acknowledge it.

The practice

Snuggle down and get yourself really cosy; make sure you'll be warm enough too. We need maximum self-nurture for this practice! We're going to explore fear; we're going to map out its ever-changing territory, its mountains and valleys, its fault lines, its cracks and crevices.

Whereabouts in your body can you find fear? What colour is it? What shade? How do you know this is fear? What's its signature, its logo? Each of us experiences a slightly different brand of fear. It comes with slightly different features, slightly different accessories.

What thoughts accompany fear? Name them, maybe even write them down. Know that they are not concrete. They may not even be true; they are 'just thoughts'.

All the while, be gentle, be tender, be soft. We don't need to stiffen and contract around fear any more. Let go of the armouring; softly whisper 'hello'.

'There is nothing to fear in fear'. It's just fear, that universal phenomenon that is most surely not unique to you. Think of it as 'the fear' rather than 'my fear'.

As you sit with fear, sitting next to it and softly whispering 'hello' to it, does it change? If so, how? Does it respond to being acknowledged? What colour is it now? Stay with it as long as feels comfortable, and beyond, if you feel resourced enough. Accompany it where it wants to go, where it wants to lead you. What is it trying to show you, to teach you?

As you come to the end of your exploration you might like to journal about it. Do this practice five days in a row and watch what happens. Treat it as a scientific experiment of the universal phenomenon called 'fear'.

Seeing through catastrophizing

A particular manifestation of fear is catastrophizing. When we are caught up in dread and terror it is very easy for the mind to spiral off and imagine the worst possible scenario, the worst possible outcome. Unfortunately, this only serves to exacerbate the situation and our sense of crisis. Here we can see the direct relationship between our levels of fear and the kind of thoughts we have. We can see clearly how our fear impacts on our thinking.

Had fear and catastrophizing taken hold, the hard lump I found in my abdomen one day could quickly have become a malignant tumour in my mind, rather than simply the unknown hard lump that it was. (It turned out to be benign fibroids in the uterus.) I did make a doctor's appointment as quickly as I could though!

Dropping down into the body

When we notice the mind assuming the worst, simply labelling this as 'catastrophizing' can be very helpful, using the 'noting' method. When you become aware that you're catastrophizing, or experiencing other overwhelming emotions, you can then drop down into the body and out of the mind. When our thoughts come with that level of emotional charge, dropping down into the body can be an enormous relief. It helps dissipate that charge. This is a good time to do the Body Scan (see p. 56). By bringing our conscious awareness back to the physical sensations in the body, back to the present moment, rather than some imagined future Armageddon, we can know that we're OK. In this very moment we are safe.

The sooner we notice we're catastrophizing the easier it is to drop out of it, to let go of it, before it runs completely rampant. What you will find is that as you practise mindfulness you will gradually be able to spot earlier and earlier when you are starting to tip into catastrophizing. You will increasingly be able to nip it in the bud.

Here is Martina's experience of catastrophizing. Notice the transformation that comes by her managing to stay with her suffering, observing it and exploring it.

Martina's story

A few years ago (I'd been practising mindfulness for about a year) I was in Rome on a meditation retreat. A few days before it started my son had left on a long and demanding cycle trip. Despite not having been very well beforehand, he hadn't wanted to follow my advice and postpone the trip. I felt the strong need to 'accompany him' in my mind and to get at least one message a day from him to reassure me that things were going OK.

One evening, while on my meditation stool, and not yet having heard from him at all, I was gripped by worry and found myself being bombarded by catastrophic thoughts and images. Added to which was my annoyance that my meditation, this precious 'me' time, was being 'disturbed' by such terrifying emotions, mixed in with feelings of guilt at being a mother incapable of protecting her own son, feelings of guilt for having let him leave. I was experiencing an almost unbearable suffering . . . when, at a certain moment, some words came to me, words which had been quoted that very day: 'Have you ever tried hugging your fear?'

Suddenly, with the word 'hugging', which made me think of a

mother hugging and protecting her son, everything changed. I too was gathered up within that embrace, as a mother; so too was the guilt, all the sense of contraction in the heart, the heaviness, the tension in the shoulders and belly. My breath was held within that hug also, which made me feel alive and able to hold all that was coming into being moment by moment in this expansive embrace. I felt an immense sense of spaciousness and love which seemed to extend to every mother and every son in the world, to all their joys and to their inevitable suffering. I won't ever forget that moment! The deep worry hadn't disappeared, it was still there, but – having welcomed it in that wide embrace – it was no longer oppressive . . . and it held an infinite tenderness.

Coping with other overwhelming emotions

In tough times a whole range of powerful emotions can shake our foundations and feel like more than we can cope with. Whatever you're dealing with – and it can change from one moment to the next in a veritable emotional rollercoaster – know that you can work with it in exactly the same way as we've worked with physical pain and fear. Essentially, we open to it, as Martina did. As gingerly as we need to, we gently step towards it, we explore it in all its florid manifestations, all the while remembering to nurture and nourish ourselves as best we can, to be compassionate towards ourselves and our suffering. We certainly don't want to be giving ourselves a hard time. Things are tough enough as it is!

In the final chapter, we'll look at how to take some of the heat out of our situation. How can we slow things down to a manageable pace?

9

Slowing the process down and surrendering to it

Slowing the process down

A defining aspect of crisis is the intensity of it. Coping with the sheer intensity can be very challenging, both for ourselves and those around us. Slowing the crisis down to a manageable pace will help to dissipate some of the intensity. This will give us some space around it and enable us to step back just enough to ease things. It will enable us to watch how everything is unfolding from the vantage point of the 'witness'.

My story
When my mother died it was sudden and traumatic. She was rushed into hospital, and she passed over about a week later. When someone dies, there's usually a great deal to do and organize in a relatively short period of time, for the funeral or celebration of life event. That's especially difficult when there's a great deal of grief and even shock to cope with.

My mother died very early on a Sunday morning. As all the offices were closed, there was nothing much we could do to obtain the death certificate, register the death, or anything else. This was all unfolding in Bournemouth, on the south coast of England, in mid-July. So my husband and I went and sat on the beach and meditated in the quiet of that early Sunday morning.

The blessing was that it enabled me to have just a little time with the enormity and intensity of my emotions. The guilt, the grief, the relief, they were all there, so raw at that point I couldn't even name them. That brief period of 'time out' gave me a little space around what was going on. It allowed me to step back a fraction before the onslaught of the busyness of making all the arrangements. Looking back, I coped with one of the hardest weeks of my life remarkably well. I'm sure the time and space we found that Sunday made all the difference.

We may not get much space around what is happening, we may not be able to step back far, but finding that little bit can be just enough to shift a situation from 'unmanageable' into 'just about manageable'.

Beans on Toast

How can we help slow things down to a manageable pace? By bringing our mindfulness practice into whatever needs doing. Establishing, or re-establishing, some simple, basic routine is very helpful when times are tough. We still need to eat; we still need to sleep. 'Doing the ordinary', even if we just fix ourselves some beans on toast, if it's done with mindfulness, helps slow things down and bring us into the here and now.

Having been in crisis myself, I know what it is, in times of need, to eat beans straight from the tin. Hopefully, if you're at home and have a toaster, it's easy enough to at least have them on toast. The point of this practice is to illustrate how to bring mindfulness into your daily activities and to give you an opportunity to try that.

As always, turn off any radios, TVs, phones and anything else that might interfere. In times of crisis and overwhelm, there is so much going on internally that all that extra stimulation may be overloading you anyway.

The practice

Before you start getting anything out of the cupboard, take a few moments, where you're standing, to feel into your body. Feel the soles of your feet on the ground, noticing the surface beneath them, maybe lino, tiles, just noticing.

If it feels a bit difficult at first to connect with your feet and the ground, try flexing your knees a little, kind of bouncing up and down, feeling the weight of your body as you do so. Bring your attention to the breath and follow a few cycles of the breath, noticing where in the body you feel the movement and sensations of the breath.

Take your time. When you feel ready, start getting the bread and baked beans out. Find a saucepan or dish for the microwave. As you do so, notice the texture and weight of the things you pick up, how they feel in your hands. Notice any sounds you make. Is there any other way you can bring in the senses? Is it fresh bread, with the wonderful unique smell of freshly baked bread?

You don't need to do things particularly slowly, but notice any tendency to want to rush. Just take your time. Notice any thoughts or feelings and let them evaporate like the steam from a kettle, coming back to the senses and the body.

Once you've got the beans on toast ready, sit down and eat them with the same level of mindfulness, the same level of attention to the senses. The main sense now will probably be taste. What do you notice? How does the first mouthful taste different from the second, from the last? Notice also the texture of the toast and beans, the contrast of the two, against your tongue, your palate. Does the juice make the bread go soggy?

Once you've finished eating you might like to journal any impressions or insights you gained.

This may not seem the most exciting of practices, but that's the whole point. We're bringing mindfulness into the everyday, into ordinary life. The more you can focus on 'doing the ordinary' – having a shower, cleaning your teeth, making simple meals – all with moment-by-moment awareness, the more you'll be able to slow things down; the better you'll be able to manage the intensity of the crisis.

The same approach and principles can be applied to any activity, remembering always to start from a connection with the body and the ground, and then focusing on the senses and how they bring you into the present moment.

Surrendering to the process

Not only do we want to be able to slow things down to a manageable pace, we also, ideally, want to be able to surrender totally to the process. We want to be able to let go, to relax into the chaos. We want to not resist, not try to struggle and fight our way out of crisis. We want to know that we are being held by something bigger than ourselves; to be able to trust that.

This ability to surrender totally to the process, to trust unconditionally, comes with practice. As we step towards our fear, explore it and discover it is essentially unfounded, formless, we start to build our trust in being here, now, with whatever arises. As we work with our pain, physical or emotional, and investigate its colours, its contours, so we discover it is ever changing, ever flowing, so we start to trust just a little bit more that this moment is an OK moment to be in. We can bear it. We can handle it. Little by little we make friends with that which horrifies us, terrifies us. We find the idea of 'relaxing into the chaos' not quite so wacky, not quite so outrageous.

The ultimate surrender of all, the ultimate letting go, is as we come towards the end of our lives. Yet whatever shape or form our crisis, our ability to surrender to it, to stop struggling, fighting, resisting, will invariably change its shape, change its form. We have a sense of freedom when we are able to stop struggling.

This moment of surrender is a moment of total mindfulness, of being right here, right now. The ultimate irony is that the moment we give up trying to make something shift, it can and it does. It is only when we stop using the mind and the ego to try to battle and box our way out of it, only in that moment of giving up, can we come through.

Make the 'This too' mantra your own

At this point I'd like to remind you of Melli O'Brien's short mantra 'This too' from Chapter 7 (p. 74). To be able to remind ourselves in the midst of the chaos of crisis that our aim is to accept it all, to accept everything, to surrender totally, is a wonderful gift indeed. As I said, have a go at adapting Melli's words to make the mantra your own. Anything that works for you or has meaning for you personally is great.

Here is my version and my invitation to you.

I surrender
I surrender
I surrender

In this moment
And in this moment
And in this

Take my hand
And we will surrender together

In this moment
And in this moment
And in this.

I hope you have been able to feel me holding your hand as I've led you through these simple mindfulness practices. Be kind to yourself, reach out for support and know that you're doing your best. May you move through this period of crisis with as little suffering as possible, with as much ease as possible. Go well on your journey.

Useful addresses and resources

Be Mindful
The Mental Health Foundation
Colechurch House
1 London Bridge Walk
London SE1 2SX
Website: www.bemindful.co.uk

The Mental Health Foundation's mindfulness resource.

Catherine G. Lucas
www.catherine-g-lucas.com

The author's website.

Maytree
72 Moray Road
Finsbury Park
London N4 3LG
Tel.: 020 7263 7070
Website: www.maytree.org.uk

A sanctuary for the suicidal in London, offering up to four nights' free accommodation and support.

Mental Health Foundation
Colechurch House
1 London Bridge Walk
London SE1 2SX
Tel.: 020 7803 1100
Website: www.mentalhealth.org.uk

A charity specializing in research and policy development, focusing on preventing mental health problems.

Sacred Space Foundation
Fell End
Mungrisdale
Cumbria CA11 0XR
Tel.: 01768 779831
Website: www.sacredspace.org.uk

Offers accommodation and support, providing peaceful and confidential rest and recuperation for those who are exhausted, stressed, burned out or experiencing a sense of crisis in life.

Samaritans
Freepost RSRB-KKBY-CYJK
PO Box 9090
Stirling FK8 2SA
Tel.: 116 123
Website: www.samaritans.org

The Samaritans' helpline is available 24 hours a day, 365 days a year.

Self Injury Support
PO Box 3740
Bristol BS2 2EF
Tel.: 0117 927 9600
Website: www.selfinjurysupport.org.uk

Resources and support for those who self-harm, including *The Rainbow Journal*, by and for young people, produced by Catherine G. Lucas.

Spiritual Crisis Network
Website: www.spiritualcrisisnetwork.uk

The organization offers information and support by email via a form on its website. It promotes understanding and support for those going through profound personal transformation. The Spiritual Crisis Network was founded by Catherine G. Lucas in 2004.

Audio recordings

'Mindful Sundays with Catherine G. Lucas' – free mindfulness audio recordings: www.catherine-g-lucas.com

Free mindfulness audio recordings, including ten-minute practices, such as the Body Scan: www.freemindfulness.org

Free mindfulness audio recordings by Catherine G. Lucas, including The Selfie Hug and Walking Meditation: www.insighttimer.com/catherinelucas

Free interviews and mindfulness masterclasses with Melli O'Brien and guests: www.mrsmindfulness.com

References and further reading

Burch, Vidyamala (2008) *Living Well with Pain and Illness: The mindful way to free yourself from suffering*. London: Piatkus.

Chödrön, Pema (2005) *When Things Fall Apart: Heart advice for difficult times*. London: Element.

Cowell, Philip (2016) *Keeping a Journal*. London: Sheldon Press.

Das, Lama Surya (2004) *Letting Go of the Person You Used to Be: Lessons on change, loss and spiritual transformation*. New York: Broadway Books.

Graham, Linda (2013) *Bouncing Back: Rewiring your brain for maximum resilience and well-being*. Novato, CA: New World Library.

Hanson, Rick (2009) *Buddha's Brain: The practical neuroscience of happiness, love and wisdom*. Oakland, CA: New Harbinger.

Kabat-Zinn, Jon (1990) *Full Catastrophe Living: Using the wisdom of your body and mind to face stress, pain, and illness*. New York: Dell Publishing.

King, Anthony P., et al (2013), 'A pilot study of Group Mindfulness-Based Cognitive Therapy (MBCT) for Combat Veterans with Posttraumatic Stress Disorder (PTSD)', *Journal of Depression and Anxiety* 30(7): 638–45.

Levine, Stephen (1997) *A Year to Live*. New York: Random House.

Linehan, Marsha (2006) 'Mechanisms of change in dialectical behavior therapy: Theoretical and empirical observations', *Journal of Clinical Psychology*, 62(4): 459–80.

Lucas, Catherine G. (2017) *Alcohol Recovery: The Mindful Way*. London: Sheldon Press.

Lucas, Catherine G. (2015) *Coping with a Mental Health Crisis: Seven steps to healing*. London: Sheldon Press.

Lucas, Catherine G. (2011) *In Case of Spiritual Emergency*. Forres: Findhorn Press.

Macy, Joanna and Johnstone, Chris (2012) *Active Hope: How to face the mess we're in without going crazy*. Novato, CA: New World Library.

Mindfulness All-party Parliamentary Group (2015) 'Mindful Nation UK'. London: The Mindfulness Initiative.

Neff, Kristin (2011) *Self-Compassion: Stop beating yourself up and leave insecurity behind*. London: Hodder & Stoughton.

Penman, Danny and Burch, Vidyamala (2013) *Mindfulness for Health*. London: Piatkus.

Rezek, Cheryl (2016) *Anxiety and Depression: The Mindful Way*. London: Sheldon Press.

Sandford, Matthew (2006) *Waking: A memoir of trauma and transcendence*. New York: Rodale.

Tolle, Eckhart (1999) *The Power of Now*. London: Hodder and Stoughton.

Wax, Ruby (2014) *Sane New World: Taming the mind*. London: Hodder and Stoughton.